Northern Prospects

Other *Your Scrivener Press* poetry:

Roger Nash, *In the Kosher Chow Mein Restaurant,*
1996.

Kim Fahner, *You Must Imagine The Cold Here,* 1997.

Roger Nash, ed. *Spring-Fever: (W)rites of Spring, 1997—
An Anthology of Poems From the Ontario Division
of the League of Canadian Poets,* 1997.

Monique Chénier, Melanie Marttila, Natalie Wilson,
NeoVerse: Northeastern Ontario Poetry, 1998.

Acknowledgements:

All poems in this volume are previously unpublished
except Marianne Schafer's "Bay of Islands Alphabet,"
which appeared in *Voices from the Bay,* published by the
Bay of Islands Community Association.

Northern Prospects
An Anthology of Northeastern Ontario Poetry

edited by
Roger Nash

Your Scrivener Press

Canadian Cataloguing in Publication Data

Main entry under title:
        Northern Prospects: an anthology of northeastern
Ontario poetry

ISBN 1-896350-07-0

        1. Canadian poetry (English)—Ontario, Northern.
2. Canadian poetry (English)—20th century.
I. Nash, Roger, 1942–

PS8295.5.O5N667 1998   C811'.54'080971313
C98-900960-2   PR9198.2.O52N667 1998

Book design: Laurence Steven
Cover art: *Snow Driven*, by John Ernsting

Published by *Your Scrivener Press*
465 Loach's Road, Sudbury, Ontario, Canada,
P3E 2R2

Contents

Anthony Armstrong

Dave Bartlett

Jennifer Broomhead

Julie Cameron

Monique Chénier

Kim Fahner

Tom Gerry

Trevor Laalo

Art Quesnel

Marianne Schafer

Mike Shain

Literary Biographies

Introduction

Roger Nash

This anthology should prove a nourishing one in meeting our natural—and universal—human hunger for the imaginative vitality of poetry. It's a tureen full of verse-soup that will really stick to your ribs. For those who enjoy savouring both soup and the tale of how the pot got to the table, here's the story.

In the winter of 1996, Your Scrivener Press grew the idea of publishing an anthology of poetry from Northeastern Ontario —Hearst to Gravenhurst, Wawa to Mattawa, and north to James Bay. Immediately, it seemed a crucial project. Northeastern Ontario is a large region. Having travelled and lived in it for over thirty years, I know it is bursting at the seams with poetic activity, in cities, hamlets, isolated lakes and lumber-camps. Yet the region has been sadly under-represented by Ontario publishers, who generally prefer the cost-effectively cosier route of publishing poets from large urban areas in the south. This is a great loss to Canadian poetry, since alternate voices go unheard, voices that often have something importantly different to say from those more shaped by homogenizing trends in large centres. Just as our economy, as operated at present, is threatening biological diversity world-wide, so it threatens a rich diversity among poetic voices, that can safeguard vitality in a poetic tradition. Besides, where is it written that, to be any good, poets must be born or live on Yonge Street? Shakespeare didn't hail from London, but from a village—what's its name?—that probably would be obscure today but for his poetry and plays. And genetics and fate placed Al Purdy in Wooler and Ameliasburg, not in downtown Toronto. Be honest, do you know where Wooler, Ontario, is?

Your Scrivener announced a Poetry Competition in the summer of 1997, seeking poets to anthologize. The competition was advertised widely in the province and region, in newspapers, journals, and on television. A wide net was cast, to bring in even hitherto entirely unknown, but excellent, poets, however remote the lake they fished on. Entrants were invited to send from five to fifteen poems, in a submission not to exceed fifteen pages in total. We were looking for poets with a body of work in which they celebrated the many moods of life. Prizes were announced (1st—$300, 2nd—$150, 3rd—$50), and an October deadline set.

Judging took place in November and December. There were one hundred and twenty submissions, many of which were at or near the limit of fifteen pages. Judging was done "blind," with no knowledge of who the poets were. Submissions came from all parts of the region. The level of writing was high, showing how rich the region is in poets. Many very promising submissions had to be returned, since the practicalities of book publishing meant only fourteen poets, at most, could be anthologized. So our advice to those who had their submissions returned is: don't be disheartened; keep writing, and enter other competitions that come along.

Here are the criteria I worked with, as competition judge. (1) Poems should have a sense of spontaneity, and not seem laboured (which is not to say it doesn't take much work and revision to achieve this!). (2) Poems should be true to life, in its ambiguities and complexities. (3) They should combat clichés and deadening over-familiarity, by exploring fresh ways of seeing things. (4) No word in a poem should be superfluous; each should play a role in shaping sense. (5) Poems should leave central parts of their sense *unsaid* directly, proceeding by an indirection that lets the reader co-create sense in making inferences and associations, taking up allusions, and so on. For a great strength of poetry lies in what it *shows*, rather than in what it *says*. (6) The form of poems should, integrally, shape their sense, and not cause a schizo-phrenic form/content division within them.

Prize-winners were announced in December: 1st prize—Lorraine Janzen; 2nd prize—Laurie Kruk; 3rd prize—Robert Dickson; Honourable Mention—Anthony Armstrong. You will find our prize-winners celebrated in the first section of the anthology. A further ten contributors to the anthology were selected in January. Our fourteen contributors speak in an impressive variety of poetic voices, showing what far-ranging territory poetry can cover. Poetry can be about anything, not just hallowed literary motifs; even about waiting, interminably, at a bus-stop.

Good poets, and their ways of writing, always have been as different as peas in a pod. If you get a room full of poets, about all they have in common—though a powerful common denominator it is—is the pod: that they write poetry. Seeing this helps smash some silly stereotypes about poets. All poets are no more alike than all farmers, or all mothers. What matters is individual mindfulness in completing the task at hand, whether it be feeding the chickens, or writing a sonnet (or, as a poet might say: feeding a sonnet and writing a chicken). As a glance at the literary biographies of our contributors will show you, poets can be of any age. You don't have to wait until that merely mythical time when you are properly "grown-up." Nor are you safely past poetry because you've retired. You don't have to have a degree; let alone a degree in English Literature. Though some poets—like many unlucky folks—are unemployed, the Muse doesn't demand unemployment from poets. Poets can be mattress-makers, lawyers, nurses, bartenders, teachers, fundraisers, soldiers, students. . . . I, myself, am a failed pig-farmer, amongst other things. Poets are wherever poetry is being made, in the many, many walks of life. Poetry is not something that happens in some cocooned area at the edge of life, occupied only by the bloodless stereotypes of poets. Seeing this, and honouring it, is a way of seeing that poetry is one of many things at the centre of life; as needed, today, in making sense of things, as it ever was in the past.

I would like to thank all entrants to the competition, for the pleasure of meeting them in their poetry; and our authors, for the instructive delight of being able to help when they revised their poems.

A last word. As President of the League of Canadian Poets, I know how lucky Northeastern Ontario is, that a new small literary press, Your Scrivener, has opened in its midst, in hard times that are causing small presses across Canada to wobble and fold. But it is just this courageous flying in the face of trends, on a shoe-string budget, that marks the spirit of many northerners. Let's support this courage in our midst. We will all—not just poets—be better for it.

discovery poems
1492-1992
I   techumseh street

walking down techumseh street
schoolbag swinging
& feet drumming the beat
of the class recitation

> *where i walk to school each day*
> *indian children used to play*

i've got one foot on the sidewalk
& the other on a dirt trail
dark woods moving in & out
between stucco bungalows
canoes on the canal

shuffling the leaves of past & present
i see footsteps everywhere
shadows so deep
you could disappear forever
hidden paths & imagined circles

i walk like my father
feet wide   heels firm
toes splayed out
i have to force my feet in
to walk these unaccustomed steps
redirect maybe 500 years
to match my stride
with these silent prints

tracking the road with another's grace
listening to another chant
as i look for ghosts on techumseh street
look not for ghosts but for children playing
& calling me to join

Janzen 14

II indian dust

opa bought the land on niagara street
made a farm with his sons   the women
hoeing planting picking sorting packing
the men driving tractor spraying fruit
loading baskets in the pickup for market

children playing all around
climbing the silo to see the farm
spread out below like a wheel
round rim of hills & creeks
white roads spoking through orchards & fields
& at the centre   the familiar farmyard circle
our house   packing shed   two houses
for uncles & aunts   tool shed   chicken coop   barn
& up a little hill opa & oma's house by the willow

circle of buildings & outlying land
my whole wheel of fortune then
family everywhere
living & working with each other
me with many parents loving & disregarding
wandering through orchards eating peaches
discarding clothes & dancing in the valley

mounding up piles of indian dust
on the farm road by our house
so i could watch the fine white cloud
rise & dissolve into blue air
when the flatbed trailer rolled through

wondering even then why we all called it *indian dust*
& thinking now we found forgotten figures
in the sand   heard the land sing of other children

Janzen 15

with many parents   other plantings & buildings
lifting their voices on earth motes in the sun
telling her tale to the sky with the delicate dance
of her dusty children & then taking them back
to her deep & careful keeping   her unending song
a handful of sand sifting the sonorous years

III hawkeye

schoolroom in port weller   hot afternoon
& rows full of kids i don't know
from the other side of the canal
dutch & english & german & native
blonde & black heads bent over books
flies buzzing in windows
or spinning in circles on the floor

outside   behind the trees   a boat travels
up the canal   siren shriek telling me
there's another waiting in the lock

            i sit & dream
of other times in this place
before concrete & print
before cold wars & fear huddled
with raised arms under desks
straightening my spine & starting to write
at the sound of precise footsteps
clicking down the hall & pausing
by our door as hawkeye examines
our silent backs   touching our work
with his fierce & sudden presence
his upright carriage   his erect head
with its bristled mohawk cut

hawkeye
carrying cultural memory for all of us
with his stern unrelenting drive   his pride
in the plaids & economy of his scottish father
the wood lore & lineage of his iroquois grandmother
teaching us to love this land & its histories
offering canada to us daily with the strength
of his body   sharp eyes flinty with anger & hope

IV new world

we jump & jump   the waves going higher   higher
rope turning & feet leaping off pavement
history reduced to a skipping song

in fourteen hundred and ninety-two
columbus sailed the ocean blue

in fourteen hundred & ninety-two my folk
sailed the ocean on whaling ships
blue-eyed sailors with deft hands hauling the ropes
tacking home to feather beds over the stove
warm with the love of wives & the smell of soup
sleeping children all around   the hearth swept
the copper polished   the world serene   *gezellig*

dutch domesticity disrupted by discovery
not of land or water or people but of language
the power of words   the way words could make
the kingdom of heaven here & now on earth
turning from rome & king & country to be
martyred over metaphors   insisting on symbols
to the last   then leaving familiar streets & canals
to farm prussian valleys   ukranian steppes
eventually   canadian prairies & niagara fruitland
a people of peace tilling the land god & king gave them
ploughing under the cossack turf
planting the indian earth
believing their labour & love   their words
could make the land their own

                over the ocean blue
                the people sang songs of harvest
                welcomed the strangers with their crops

thinking earth & sky were big enough
rivers wide enough for all to travel

a leap of faith   the turning rope & the arched body
jumping into air   looking for thanksgiving
hoping to land with grace in a peaceable kingdom

Janzen 19

V indian summer

light on the water in hot october
sun in the wind after frost
boats off the bank riding gray waves
& clouds writing the autumn sky
traces of dead summer in port dalhousie
tumbled stalks bleached with the sun
or dark with decay blaze with chrysanthemums
& scarlet yew berries   bright leaves tossing
grapes red & white on the vine

digging the cold wet earth
pressing in bulbs   my fingers
find traces of other travellers
white grub squirming   squirrel's nut
snail coiled in its mottled shell
fragment of blue & white china
red brick   medicine bottle   4" spike
stones & roots & centipedes
worms tunnelling   turning over the layers

uncovering the years   dis-
covering what i can
i wonder what i would find
if i could dig deep enough
reach far enough with my planting
waiting the long winter
for flowers to shake off the snow
for red & yellow flames under the sun
& purple-black petals in the wind

talking vulva

so vagina means sheathe
latin slang turned bio-medical
proper word for improper body part

imagine the roman soldier
the morning after
groping for his sword
for his word for the experience

a sheathe for a sword
a scabbard for a weapon
it fits so well
like a gun in a holster
like a hand in a glove
like anything whose
function is secondary
whose meaning is relative
to some really BIG THING

wrap this around your tail
we're talking vulva
& this speaking flesh
around your rib
this wound
bleeds   beats   bears
whether you
are here
or not

Janzen 21

graveyard tunes
for pat friesen

hi ma
just thought i'd call
haven't talked in awhile
wanted to let you know—
that saturday before you died?

—i was playing hookey from death

thinking maybe if i drove far enough into alien landscape
i wouldn't see death at every corner thumbing a ride

i know. never pick up a stranger. but ma i knew this guy
or thought i did. what do you ever really know anyway
a name   a face   a gesture   an implied history maybe
like a half-remembered melody you find yourself hum
ming   a reverberating chord   enharmonic echo

so i picked him up en route to nowhere
he had his own voice to haunt him
eyes to compel him   death to discover or deny

we travelled together the length of a march afternoon
your last saturday. what did the ceiling   the walls look like
after so much living   so much life
a silent room   an empty bed   a closed window

where did we go? you'll never believe it ma
i played hookey from death
by wandering through a graveyard
sleet drumming us with icy fingers
headstones lined up like black keys
two strangers looking for a stranger's grave

Janzen 22

among rows of death indiscriminate
a hundred years & more of dying
under the spruce trees
he coughing & wrapped in a muffler
me blowing my nose   losing my hat
wishing for warmth & wisdom
for a manual   a guide   a mother

we make our way to the place
the wind a knife through the heart
snow on the flat stone
stark letters   a date
an etched keyboard   middle c

so little to sum up a life pat said
so little i thought to mark a death

are you laughing ma?
the music's too loud   i can't hear you

Janzen 23

Charlie and Elsie

Maternal grandmother, Elsie Hill,
Irish maid newly planted:
Rockglen, Saskatchewan, 1927;
living under my great-granny's roof,
got appendicitis, blew up
like a bloated cow
and asked young master Charlie,
"Did you *do* something
the other night?"

He didn't accept her accusation, didn't
even believe in kissing—"swapping spits
and catching colds," he called it—
but, as a fresh CCF-er, felt sorry
for the Irish working girl,
islanded on the burnt-yellow prairie,
and married her. A step up for Elsie, he thought it,
and grand gesture, promising more,
for an idealist farmer. Except that the Depression,
which drew up cod and catfish together in its net,
rudely removed them from hope, leaving their plans
high and dry, without spawn.
(Except for my mother and aunt, solemn-faced daughters.
Soon after Betty came, they sold up;
moved to Windsor, Ontario. Traded horse and buggy
for Ford and GM.)

But Elsie never forgot that earlier island,
kept escaping back
to its social servitude. An annoyed,
genteel-poor family

always sent her "home. To your husband."

Married life became a contest. Anniversaries
should be marked with black arm bands, Elsie declared.
Once she threw potatoes (uncooked)
at her silent husband,
in raw Irish anger.
And left Charlie three times,
the last just before illness
drove her back to his door, age 64. Cancer
devoured her bowels, seat of the passions. Still,
she passed on to one grandchild
her love of poetry, passion
which served her for wind-break
through life's Canadian weathers.

Charlie lived to be ninety-eight, devoted New Democrat
and still spry on his bike in the eighties,
until a wobbly left turn
into the swing of a bus, denied him the dignity
of meeting fate on his feet, like a boxer.
Instead, his last years found their focus
resisting over-worked nurses' cajoling,
tuning out his roommate's
day-long prayers to Doris,
another lost wife.

With visitors, Charlie good-naturedly guessed
at names and ages, strained to recount the story
of an ill-timed horse trade
from the most hopeful days of his life,
his young manhood and marriage.

He never mentioned
the woman who shared those years, learning

a bitter foreign soil
and beside whom he would eventually be planted,
filling a space waiting over thirty years
for that last pioneer—

belatedly, belying sentiment
but keeping up his end
of the bargain;
like the mare
he struggled to keep and feed
in an arid climate.

His constancy his legacy
—begat out of pride, necessity, sweat—
and the many Loyalist reticences
his granddaughter here
struggles to undo.

When Her Thighs Were Perfect

Well, once
they were measured
in hot quick glances
from sun-gilded cars
booming hormonal thunder.
Artemis, the huntress:
she could walk on those legs
right out of herself,
dizzy with breath,
opening the new page
on agonizing drives home,
in sticky lingering embrace
of a cranked-down bucket-seat;
marathon petting sessions
in her parents' driveway,
or the parking lot
of a "Kiss and Ride."
Tiny gold leg-hairs
tingling, pre-razor,
flesh finger-smudged.
She still carries
the shadow of bliss
that seared her,
first bristly male kisses,
hands climbing knee—
before she slammed
the passenger door,
almost four. Smoothed
down her shorts,
erasing. Then the hall
light came on, and her father
put his slippered foot
on the stair.

Fifteen years later, she learns to read
a new chapter of travel and time,
mapping her flesh with "You Are Here."
Future destinations
pointed out by her sisters, moving on with
or without drivers. Asphalt waiting,
and the father's vigil, over;
the whole road is now hers.

Yet when blushes are only applied with brushes
and she is sealed against the ritual quills
of husbands out for the evening, howling
with the pack that turns against hunters
at the goddess's whim, she aches
for an untouched page
to turn over, embracing
its muteness. Settles instead
for the lab report, brought
like a bouquet of roses by knowing lovers

declaring all negative.

Kruk 28

on the treadmill

6 a.m.
A crow rasps ownership over the suburb,
towering pines that top the house,
soon to be handed over to the new occupants
and plans of pruning.

My father coughs, and on the other side of the house,
I roll out of dreaming. June is for brides. Today is their ghost
anniversary—the thirty-seventh they never saw, together.
So he vows to add thirty-seven
to his seventy, despite the cough, and the dizziness
that stops him in his tracks, on regular walks
round the neighbourhood he watched grow
from rows of matchstick trees and raw yards
with blond children sitting in kiddie pools.
Now quick foreign chatter, warm colours, strange
gatherings of whispering fabric, passing him on the sidewalk,
spice its Wonder Bread blandness. His aching lungs,
tight chest, preserving, as he gasps, the faint
scent of saffron.

He rises, dresses in yesterday's shirt—sweat glands
have dried up this year—and goes downstairs
for the glass of orange juice he left out last night,
so the burst of citrus won't freeze his fillings.
Little shocks must be avoided now.

Ghosts track him through the house—of children,
shrieking assaults on the furniture and one another.
Of teenagers, sprawling on the floor, whispering
laughter, *Oh my Gods*, phone nested
in their unwashed hair. Of lovers on the couch,
winding around each other and waves of Queen,

Styx, Elton John. ("Someone saved my life tonight.")

This afternoon, the second stress test.
A girl with green fingernails has him step
onto a treadmill. After five leaden minutes, she stops him:
success or failure? Breath returning, verdict deferred. The
    doctor
will call him next week, she says, unrolling
a stick of gum. He drives home, legs trembling
at every red. Late that night, as he wrestles
with sleep, he still feels the pull he must resist,
force of the machine tugging
against watery muscles. Floor rolling,
running, jumping. Stealing his strength, his maleness,
his youth. Lungs aching, sweat seeping. Edge creeping ever
    closer,
teasing his heels with dark oceans,
as he cries out. His wife's name, ex-named now, from some
lost day of islands, soft hands. Clutches instead
the corner of the mattress and
another long day is launched
in the hoarse dark mocking
sheltered by the trees he had planted.

Weighty Baggage

it is not wise to leave baggage in your car
even locked on the street in front of your
hotel   it's a crime to feel too tired
to carry too-heavy bags thru a
too-dark hotel up three flights of stairs
to a room with three too-saggy beds but
it's still a shock to see the shattered window
and the big bag gone and only vaguely a relief
to realize the ladrones
were surely in too
much of a hurry &
in the dark &
missed the plane tickets &
credit cards we couldn't
find the strength to lug in

the comandante and the sergente of the
guardia civil were much more so than
many public servants i try not to remember
or others i can't seem to forget especially
sometimes in my sleep
submachine guns levelled at my chest
in spanish border towns
by smirking men in three-cornered hats
their colleagues nudging each other
at the tables of sidewalk cafés hats off
guns on tables   belt-buckles shining
like broken glass in the sun

covered by guns   not by insurance

It's Easy (a remembrance)

is it all so easy as it seems so easy
questions or statements sign here
this won't hurt is your copy
strictly routine necessary paperwork you
report it we file it   your hand shakes
(tension surely not guilt)
the cold perhaps all of a sudden
it's cold   winter obviously (apparently) you
don't realize aren't conscious your cheeks are rosy you
are hanging on to the back of a cutter great snorts
of frozen horse breath the good smell of straw &
shit you are young & brave &
the poor farmer's forbearance is way
beyond you   anyway you get to school
you were briefly free &
perhaps dreamed of
circumnavigation, empire, cap et épée
(you had a flashlight, a room, a blanket
a book, were brave)   learned
to pronounce europe with difficulty, with
your mother, seeing dreaming beyond the pond
and a half-mile maybe of river (where is it?)
(far) (under the covers with the flashlight &
far) & when you get there again &
again & far is it so far &
even with tickets to go back (back?)
it seems not far but is it all so
easy so far so easy?

An Apartment

the apartment is not on the mountain or the sea-shore
though both are visible and near
there is no central heat here   when it's cloudy
or raining drops of moisture stay all day
on the tiled walls of kitchen & bathroom
on the sliding doors to the balcony
on sunny days windows and doors are left
open   bang shut at will   there is time
to bask or compulsively clean
the luxury of choice
life moves slowly as a horse walking
beside a man down a street past a market
the cart seems heavy the man in no hurry

villagers try on leather jackets
women buy new knives while the
men drive to the cafés

A New Knife

bought in the street market for a fair price
cool winter sun   a horse pulling a loaded cart
walks beside his man down the street
churros & tapas for sale from a trailer
we also buy sewing scissors they may
cut hair as well but paper is not good
for them   i feel spanish steel when the
knife slices thru a carrot and
the ball of my thumb
it is the sharpest knife i have used
in years   i cut my thumb only once
proof of the steel's temper
and/or mine

A Monday Morning

head & sky & paper surprisingly clear the poem
begins with the poem not the idea
of the poem
this poem is about home is
where the where is my heart
is   bright sky like a new week
like a monday morning thru
sparkling snow to school eyes
bright on the lookout for a
horse & cutter   hey here comes one now
early hitchhiking free ride to learning
(remember circumnavigation for the test)

Going Somewhere

gone they're gone all gone far
(you did too, admit it)
who went farther think father
do sounds, smells, turn your head do
distances (leisurely drives thru stony
mountain passes) give you pause does
time (even down-time) hang heavy &
do you know where you're headed do
you sometimes ever want to turn
turn turn

And Even Earlier

only retrospectively does it seem strange to have
grown up on a river called credit
merchants at the river's mouth staking
trappers to their winter needs (few wants?)
around the time of the farmers' revolt

but it is 1949 & i'm sitting between charlie
overland & sam dunnage in stanley park
(not vancouver: this is erin on the credit)
& the horses (were they old? shiny with sweat?)
breathe out clouds of cold breath, go slow so
the men can get down (no rush) & saw
thru the thick ice & with big tongs
extract big blocks & later store them with
sawdust in the icehouse & in summer deliver them
sweating to the icebox in our porch

my mother paid cash when she could

Breakaway

two boards nailed to the handle of a broken
hockey stick makes a snowplow three or four
snowplows make a rink on the pond on the
credit we lace our skates on in the
kitchen   tiptoe thru the porch past the
icebox slide down the hill on our bums
& we are there & it is everywhere
for a while   the rocket & gordie howe
& teeder kennedy live on the credit &
watch out for léo boivin he hits hard & after
a thaw & a freeze we chase pucks for miles

limping back heroically on great occasions
after 2 goals 3 assists & a puck on the ankle
knocking off the snow near the sweaty ice-
box   the snowplows just as precious as the
hockey sticks & so to supper & so to bed
brave books under the covers until the
final order   then dreams of championships
& escapes from sweaty dungeons breaking the
chains   skating down the river to forever
(maybe to europe, that new word)

Dickson 38

Assorted Observations Jn & Around Sant Carles (with a nod to frank davey)

the teenaged girls dressed in black strangely resemble
their grandmothers but the hairdos & gum are a dead
giveaway. except for cafés & restaurants, most businesses,
as well as schools, are closed from one to four. more or
less. the most popular cigarettes seem to be Marlboros.
some older men still smoke black tobacco, costing less
than half the price. fish & shellfish are fresh, abundant &
relatively inexpensive. many table wines, & some
estate-bottled wines (non-vintage) cost less than a
dollar. people in the market are quite friendly. you
may taste cheese before buying. you are often given a
tangerine to try. when you ask for 2 kilos, some vendors
will offer you a deal on 5. you may find them very ripe.
locally grown delta del ebre rice is delicious, especially in
paellas or zarzuelas. unpolished natural rice is only
available at the health food store, at health food store
prices. some local people are natural redheads. many
speak french: for years a number of catalans have worked
on the grape harvest in france. english language reading
material is scarce. time (international edition), the
london times & 2 other british dailies are available
in the papeteria in the market square. there is also a
small selection, 5 or 6 titles, of paperbacks.
there is 1 copy of farley mowat's never cry
wolf in the german edition.

Downtown On The Weekend

we would skate all the way downtown
along the river, its ponds, channels bordered
by bulrushes, boots tied together over our
shoulders for the weekend hockey game on
the downtown pond, all toques & yells
& leafs & canadiens sweaters, an odd assortment
of hockey socks & artfully taped sticks reinforcing
breaks & cracks. norman rockwell canadiana. before
slapshots, before t.v. always at least one kid doing the
foster hewitt play-by-play as he played. where did
he get the breath? strutting or limping up the main
street afterwards, hot chocolate at haberman's
restaurant, the straight walk home. before girls,
pimples, self-consciousness, alcohol. the nicknames
simple, direct, perhaps mean: donkey, goop, boney,
dickey-bird (guess who?)

no mum, it doesn't hurt. then why are you limping?
not much.

Some Imports In Sant Carles De La Rapita

portuguese beer, french cheese, swiss butter.
marlboros. canned corn on the cob from canada.
the london times, time international, die telegraf.
the spanish language. renaults & peugeots.
japanese electronics, peruvian tapestries.
even catalan wine, in a way (greeks & romans).
arabic script, jewish thinkers.
kiwi fruit. california raisins. potatoes.
me.

Anthony Armstrong

I hang on the cross of your beauty
I am pinned by my longing for you
my heart is a bird with no legs
my heart is a shirtless tatoo

in a riot of leaves
in a cloud of exhaust
you showed me three ways
to get off a cross:
    like a thief
    like a thief
    and like a perhaps god

now old friends see a phantom
an old lover does too
and I've lost whatever charm it was
that got me to you

but if this is just another cross
I'll be more careful when I choose
until I'm god enough to handle
these resurrection blues

Lord,
am I your child?

then bathe me in a flood,
instruct me with lightning,
age me with your presence;

scare the shit out of me;
for I have not knelt in twenty years
and then
it was to a woman.

since you left:

I've committed half a suicide
I've tortured an ocean
I've perfected my limp

I've said two prayers:
I prayed that you'd come back to me
I prayed that you wouldn't

already,
one of my prayers has been answered

there's a feeling
I get in my gut
that tells me
my soul must live there

it's as warm
as the flesh of a tumour
as cold
as the fist of her stare

and on nights such as this
when I feel it
when I'm breathing
both water and air

I curl up
in the lap of confusion
to nurse
at the breast of despair

When You Married Me, Did You Know That You'd Get Christmas Cards Like This?

Judy says
we have free will;
I say
we have its illusion.

Judy selects
the wine;
I drink
from the bottle,
and tell her
choose to fly.

You can see her
there at the heart
of that gallery of clouds;
she had no choice—
she had to prove me wrong.

you make me feel
like Mary Magdalene
for there must have been a day
that she came to him with water
when he only wanted shade

and I am sure
he had a parable
that convinced her to remain
but *you*
gave to me a blueprint
and the memory of rain

David Bartlett

Cleaning up the bookstore

The first hour of the morning,
with only one customer,
leaves a vacuum that
I fill with the broom
and dustpan.

Making a clean sweep of it,
as it were, getting swept up
in my work, the mind wanders.

I am swept across wide
skies by clean keen cold winds,
far from the puffs of dust
I try with all my might
not to raise with the broom.
Ah, the broom, perhaps
that's where the flight comes in—
witchery—and why not, standing
here among so many spells and
sorcelments contained between covers.

It's not just the floor I clean
but the pathways through the magic.
I am the guide, the cleaner of the way,
broom in hand, perhaps with an Irish
warsong on the tape—maybe it's
jazz—depends how sophisticated
I feel. But then—with a dying fall—
it's only a part-time job and it's
a humble occupation. I sweep, I
sweep, I dump the dust.

Raven

Ravens lift off from
the side of the road
fly in front of the truck.
Wings, then all
turn white
in sunlight
reflected from
black glossy
feathers.

Between times: Georgian Bay

The rocks . . .
cracked, crushed, tossed playfully
as though some giant wayward glacier-child
dragged icy fingers
through the rocks, threw them in the air,
made sparks fly banging them together,
then left them strewn: upthrusts, outcrops, boulders, islands.

As wind cleans water, water cleans rock,
mind tends myth, myth keeps matter
in check, in order,
that we can live by water,
clear water, green water,
on rock, pink rock, rusty rock.
Our stories and songs give permission
to these lives, this place, until
some giant elemental child . . .

Mackenzie Boat Outing, September 18

Teslin strip boat—made in Yukon.
Yamaha 9.9—made in Japan.
Up-river ducks take off along right shore.
Yellow leaves on shrubs on both banks.
Cold grey waters of the Mackenzie East Channel.
Low mud banks then green grass
then driftwood then brown bunches of grass.
Spots of sunshine on the shoreline.
Black spruce tops poke above
shoreline shrubbery undergrowth.
Odd creek mouth opens up.
Check the nets . . .
She pulls hers across the bow—
float-line closest lead-line furthest.
All she got was jack.
Tundra whistling swans overhead, two pairs:
two head south, two north,
long necks leading—wings whistle.
Low clouds—like fog only freezing.
Grey waters.
Three humans in a boat.

Railway

The Ottawa, Arnprior, and the old Georgian Bay—
ain't no more nothin' being hauled out that way,
'cause the tracks have been torn up, the ties dragged away—
it just stopped makin' money, at least that's what they say.

They hauled out the timber, they shipped in the wheat.
They built towns for the workers with brightly lit streets.
Two ribbons of steel, now a few flecks of rust;
the lives and the railway just two kinds of dust.

When I was a young man, I worked by the Bay
on the trains and the freighters that came in each day.
Then I made munitions for a war far away.
When the line finally shut down, I chose to stay.

The years they passed quickly, as they always seem to.
The highway took over what this railway could do.
And all the old trainmen, I bid them adieu.
Then they made it a trail for bikes and skidoo.

You can follow the roadbed, you can ford all the streams.
It's a hole in the forest, a faint track through my dreams.
It's just bones of old commerce, the stuff of old schemes.
And I'm just an old man and don't know what it means.

Radio

" . . . if you can't find love, you've still got the radio . . ."
(Nancy Griffiths)

When wife and daughter died,
he went a bit insane,
heard voices from the radio,
listened.
It wasn't overt—dead wife,
daughter, or God—just radio
voices like doing the news.

And his old girlfriend wanted
to help,
so she took off clothes,
wound herself in antenna
wire, plugged herself into
the tuner.

As she slowly waved
her arms like
kelp in the current,
voices came
from the speakers
like slow caresses.

He entered,
saw her offer,
placed headphones
over ears,
plugged into
the amplifier, made
love to her slowly
as soft sounds
and
sex wafted through
the ether.

Relax,
radio.

Bartlett 54

Jerry Garcia

When I heard Jerry Garcia was dead,
I was outside the Mike's Mart
waiting for nine year olds Emma and Sylvia
to get a Slurpee.

Instant picture of a lonely hospital
emergency ward or addiction centre
with some nurse or orderly thumping
and pushing on his fat chest,
grey beard and curly white hair hanging
back, lolling over to one side, naked,
looking old without his glasses.

I was in the hospital this morning too,
to get a mole cut off—old friend
of my left hand for 35 years—I
can't remember it earlier than that.

Our dreams and our goals stay young,
founded in youth; our bodies grow old,
bounded by youth.

Another time my brother lost a
finger in a conveyor belt accident,
the same finger and joint *he* was missing.
My brother was a guitar player of very
local renown, it could have meant
more, could have devastated him
greatly, but he bore it well. "Hasn't
hurt Garcia any. . ."

The connections are thin—I wasn't
even that big a fan—an album or

two—a song or three remembered
and played—certainly not
a Dead Head by any stretch.

Old man, at 53 you seemed less like
those other rock gods and more
like my grandfather, human and fallible.
Have a good trip to the other side.

Jennifer Broomhead
The Bus Stop Poems

I

At the bus stop
in the field,
I feel exposed.

Everyone who drives by
can see me,
and they know what I'm doing.
I can't run for cover
because there is no cover.

Their eyes gloat as they
cruise by in their
lemons and luxury
sedans, because they
are driving
and I
am waiting.

II

So there I am at the bus stop.
I'm getting impatient: it's late
and I'm (as always, you know
me) in a hurry.

So there I am,
waiting,
pacing,
learning how to walk again,

and it's taking so long that I start
thinking.
(I hate when that happens.)

I think about you
and I think about
yesterday and I think
about tomorrow
and then
I think about you and me and yesterday
and you and me and tomorrow
and then
I don't want to think about
anything anymore
so I start to dance a jig.

III

Sometimes,
(most of the time)
I listen to music as I wait.
I (usually) do that to
isolate
myself and keep the
world out.
But . . .
there are times
when I decide to share
my music with everyone else
at the bus stop.

Sometimes,
it's just a faint
(annoying)
buzz buzz,

enough so that they know
I'm listening to
something,
but they just can't figure out
what.

Sometimes,
it's a lot louder.

Sometimes,
I don't share the sound at all.
Instead,
I share the rhythm.
I dance
and hop and
move and groove
and I can read jealousy
on the faces of the
others at the bus stop
because they want
to have fun too.

IV

At my bus stop,
there's this couple.
They're young.
They look young and in love.

They make me sick.

V

A guy's sitting (waiting)
on the bench next

to me.
He's sucking on a
tootsie roll.
By the time our
bus shows up,
it's little more than
a stick.

VI

On the bus,
there's this other couple.
They sit in front of me,
in plain view.

He holds her hand,
their fingers mesh.
He kisses her forehead,
she melts into his shoulder.
He caresses her arm,
their eyes meet.

I can still remember
that feeling.
That feeling of wanting to be
so close
to another person.
To touch them,
to be touched.

I turn away.

VII

There are moments when I'm sitting on the bus and I catch

these deep, insightful thoughts floating around in my head.

Like, maybe I want to be a nomad because my family has lived
    in the same place for so long.

My grandfather and grandmother,
my mom and dad,
uncles and aunts and countless cousins
have lived in the same town
their entire lives.

Me, I want to get out,
see the country, see the world,
meet people and do stuff.

VIII

Two or three times now,
I've run into the male
half of the lusty
couple that annoys me so.
We even talked about time, once.
Every time I see him I
smile to myself,
because he has no idea
I've written a poem about him.
(The irony of this poem does not escape me. I know that now
    he lives in two poems . . .)

IX

At the terminal
there are TEENAGERS:
Catholic school boys in identical
pressed pants and dirty sneaker-shoes;

Catholic school girls in
long socks and wide-belt skirts.
They laugh, scream, screech, yell.
They annoy me.
They fascinate me.

I was *never* that young.
I know I was never
that *young.*
I'm sure I
was never *that* young!

(Was I *ever* that young?)

X

One year ago,
I walked a different walk
to a different stop.
I was thinking of a different person
as I sat on a different bus.

Time plinks away
as I drop my quarters;
and I think about what a difference a year makes.

Things are different, yet they're
still the same.

Broomhead 62

captured

i've clambered down the bank
to photograph the river
its soothing waters
have called me from
my place on the path to venture in
and document its beauty

no one knows i am here

wet snow clings to tree trunks
their limbs stretch
to mingle with those
of other trees
a web of branches
traps the light
and the river is dark

i could fall in   drown   be swept away

muddy moss sticks to stones
their smooth surfaces
are suspiciously slippery
i lose my grip
the photograph blurs
images flow by me
as the river flows around me

and no one would ever know

Architecture

It is interesting to watch you build our house
your sweeping water turrets climbing
into a sky you have already painted
with your bruised petal words
and an issue of patched stones

Do you ever wonder what kind of house
I could build with this
with this crab's blood
and these grass widows as my workers
I would travel my hand
across the landscape that is you
and I would build you a tower of your very own
in it I would put a naked chair and
a complete stain of canvas so you
could fill every blue scratch
with a vibration of a particle
with a mood that is mine

"These are your rooms" you say
travelling your hand across a lake I have never seen
"and you will be happy here"
your convictions are an uncertain moon before me
I go quietly into these tidy rooms and inhabit them
so you may be an architect
and my skin a building before you

but I fill these rooms
these rooms that you touch
with a blueprint
for everything that's sacred.

paris when it's naked

half a block away
a moth confesses
to a single naked bulb
like a mythmaking angel
staggering to the oracle again
i tell it i don't know you
as sleeves touch and we cross over
through a puddle
and a foreign light
it's not cold but i'm getting there
and you
dazzled by every curiosity shop
and smoke filled bar
on our way back to
some distant room
where we might have met before
and i am mesmerized by
the light and rain coupling
on the pavement
a beautiful woman passes
and i could swear to her
that i never knew you
your arm suddenly surrounds me
a reckless taxi passes
the vacant witness
to an unhurried kiss
sheltered by the singed wing
burning on the altar

He Watches Her in the Swing

I loved you most
when you were in the swing.
Nighttime was the blanket
that most loosened
your delicate tongue, and I
would risk the stab of your toes
just to hear you speak
of your mother the moon.

(Years ago,
you peeled an orange,
anointed your ankles
and braided your hair.
The scent of you
lingered on
our marriage bed.)

I am standing in front of you
(inches from your bare
toes) as witness
to the stories
fastening their teeth
to your fingers.
The marks like slivers
under your nails
from writing it all down.
And the church bells at night

(the wedding and the feast)
as you turned
your gaze past me
up to the sky,
as the swing

Cameron 66

rocked every confession
from you

and your savioured tongue.
The weariness
of your immunity as
your body curved

into a bow that
slipped through the air
in a continuous arc,
while the night moths
gathered up the words
kept in a cave,

and distilled a wine
that will never grace
my hand.

The chains groaned under
your weight.
Your skirt fluttered behind

trying to catch you.

How The Men Lost Their Bacculum*

A few quick turns with the vaginal wrench
broke it into smaller pieces.
A woman used her tongue
to suck the little bones out
and swallow them.
The man was too busy enjoying it
to notice.
This is what the term 'spineless' really refers to.
This is how the men lost their spines.

* A bacculum is a small bone in the penis of all male mammals, except humans. There is no anthropological reason for this.

Cameron 68

blue petals

raining
it is the same today as the day i left
standing here now
roof crumbling
boards rotting
how many times
did i run into this field
to cry among the cornflowers
weeds you called them
when i brought you that first bouquet
wilting already
those blue petals
fell softly to the floor
and in between
how many seasons
and how many nights
were marked by
sobbing
broken dishes
and slammed doors
i would run into the fields
away from this house
that stands before me
away from you
funny
but i still remember which bowls
and which glasses broke

Cameron 69

Monique Chénier

wild woman of gogama

in winter
when she is not here
she haunts the river
her mind weaves fog circlets
over the water's edge
that is hard as bone
her feet imprint the sand
that is covered white

each spring she comes
tears her skirt to fronds
her hands to bleeding hearts
surveys her landscape shaded
by trees of thawing blood
by leaves of sun-warmed skin

her blood
her skin

each spring she eats fiddleheads
stews them up with robin-egg blue
catches flies between her teeth
discovers orchids beneath the fir

in summer she drinks
rivers stained by berries
others pick
wears hats straw-coloured faded
dresses of other times
runs wounded kites
over the flowers of gardens

Chénier 70

celebrates the solstice
with dreams
of never leaving
hides in her green world under
the hands of ferns

each fall her heart breaks
drops off like falling leaves
is cold-ripened like berries
of mountain ash

in winter she eats store-bought
tears her gaze from this
landscape
returns skirt mended hands scarred
to managed time-people
gas-heated dwellings

in winter
when she is not here
her mind is haunted
by fog circling water
footprints in the sand
and orchids under fir

slivers

cold slivers hot breath
freezes words not spoken
white and blue and yellow sparkle
on frozen fences
sun splintering the fog
behind petrified
ghostly trees

emily carr

what totems would she have drawn
in oils had she lived here
ours must be imagined
spirits fly
must be drawn from memory
totems are only for those who stay
people come and go here
take gods with them when they leave

who would have walked with her
have sat and watched her paint
been her sophie her biggest friend
tried to make the trunks here seem larger
carved totems in the burning smelters
of smouldering virgin pines
called her klee wyck even when she was sad

what woman carved in living cedar
eagle-breasted
shadowed eyes
lips caught in siren song
would have called her further into our forests
until she knew how to paint the silence
draw our woods in oil spires
in rising swirls of jagged pines

still-shot morning

mist swirls in effort
grey at first
then soft yellow folding
into the lake's temporary impenetrability
up to the sky's shifting sense of itself
instant moment of morning's indecision
still-shot before someone walks across the lens
moves water
foot-bare thoughts circling widening
until the camera must change perspectives
revealing the day

Kim Fahner

ambrosia of the gods

on the floor of your ceiling,
high above our heads,
some woman stomps out
the direction of her destiny.

not realizing that her army boots
beat out a rhythmic staccato tattoo
so that bottom dwellers wonder
at their own futures.

rain tonight,
like weeping before death,
so you offer me a ripe mango.
tell me it's ambrosia of the gods
and not to worry; all will be well.

still, beyond these walls,
plaster sconced and painted,
the storm rages and drowned ladybugs
float down the street to the port of Montreal.

Diva

The fat woman sings opera
in the early morning hours,
just when I'm trying to wake up.

Passionate selections from
Puccini and Wagner or
whatever happens to strike her fancy.
This morning she's
pretending to be Bellini's Norma.
(At least that's what
the radio announcer tells me.
So I believe her, because I'm not really
what you'd call an opera connoisseur.)

It's Bellini this morning,
as I'm driving through the rain
on a day that's really too cold
to be legitimately born of May.

Bellini.

If you say it slowly,
let it roll around on your tongue,
taste the cadence of it,
the name begins to sound
(oddly enough)
like some exotic Italian pasta.
Risotto, maybe. Or penne. Perhaps even tortellini.

Like how, when you were little,
you'd say a word over and over and over again,
until it seemed to dissolve its meaning
right in front of your eyes.

Fahner 76

So I try
to match voice and image,
to give meaning to the opera at hand,
even though
I can't begin to pretend
that I understand Italian.
(Especially since I've been known
to burn rigatoni when I'm in a rush.)

Fahner 77

geranium rain

is so often
mistaken for
something else,
like the purple dew
of lilacs
in early june,
or the damp bloom
of a peony-in-waiting.

it is the scent
that hangs
too seductively
in the bright air
of twilight;

the taste that
just barely sits on
the tip of a tongue,
with blushing lips
curled softly up
in the semblance of
an unexpected kiss
on a rainy night.

shades of moon-silver
and liquid mercury
mark the barometer
of the heart,
painting frescoes
in the mind's eye
and then
watching them,
too slowly,
too painfully,
dissolve in the
cold mist of blue
geranium rain.

Fahner 78

in utero

babies blooming like potted plants,
spheres of spirit gleam bone white
in the bellies of passing women.

i search out lost faces,
knowing they refuse to be found,
unless in some other incarnation.

and now, just me,
walking down wellington
with nostalgia in my eye.

won't even blink
for fear of dislodging the past,
shattering perspectives that would
suddenly drift into a
brightly violent kaleidoscope
of sheer uncertainty.

prefer blind illusion as a diversion
that defines the edges of this afternoon;
shadowy feathers of future tickle my fancy
and i begin to think of chrysanthemums.

metaphorical love

hedging his bets,
he writes letters of tomorrow
but sends them today.

a murder of crows
woke her this morning;
let her ride on their
feathered coal-black backs.

took her
down under
to some other country,
where stars shine
only in the heart
of another
who has foolishly
mistaken her
for a poet.

Fahner 80

Sanskrit

The day's plans,
written in Sanskrit
and mapped in the scent of
last night's curried cauliflower,
were carefully pre-ordained.

Now, faced with the
single trumpet voluntary
and bagpipe laments
at Notre Dame,
their certainty blurs
next to the stark image of
that pale painted angel
who holds a papier-maché globe
in the crook of a world weary elbow.

Silence is gilded here,
bronzed like baby shoes,
silvered with grace,
adrift on the backs of prayers
now rising towards the blue dome
that seems to speak of sky and sun.

I finally weep.

Navy Hall, Niagara River, May 30, 1995

The water wouldn't have been this chemically shocked
    turquoise
200 years ago when she was camping here at Navy Hall.
Youngstown's water tower across the wide river now
wouldn't have been there. Perhaps a few log houses
owned by cousins, brothers and sisters even, they say, family
separated not only by water then as now, but by the
    revolutionary war.
The tree line of willows, alders, chestnuts and maples, though,
would have looked much the same: all the way left,
    downstream,
along the far shore to Fort Niagara at the river's mouth.
No customs and immigration formalities in her day, crossing,
    only uneasiness
about landing on newly-revolted, newly-foreign soil.
Nevertheless, she lingered long enough there with her
    sketchbook,
found a vantage point, gazing back to here,
to draw with pen and ink, and paint
the mighty river, the tents and cabin they called Navy Hall.

Minnows—baby trout, bass—make their way against the
    current,
strangely, towards the waters of Lake Ontario. A big anti-
    clockwise eddy
is circling offshore from this dock, and the minnows have to
    struggle
to swim downstream towards their imagined destination.
The inscription carved in the stone obverse of the Simcoes'
    monument,

statuary erected in 1952 beside the refurbished Navy Hall, says:

> Here at Niagara on Sept. 17, 1792
> he presided over the first
> representative assembly
> of this province. . . .
> He brought courage to the hearts
> of the early settlers and led them
> to carve a civilization out of a
> wilderness ■ In all this he was
> unfailingly helped by his wife
> Elizabeth Posthuma Gwillim

In his naming of dozens of places in the colony,
the Governor, as Mrs. Simcoe called him, retained Niagara,
St. Lawrence, Ontario, Chippewa, Erie, names already here—
but not Toronto. He imported York, Five-Mile Creek, Ten-
    Mile Creek,
Twenty-Mile Creek, Georgiana/London, Lake Simcoe (after
    his father, he said),
the Thames River, Charlottesville, even Gwillimbury.

Being rowed around in the Governor's boat, massive Union
    Jack draped astern,
she drew the hills and waters and rocks, the looming dark
    forests.
As she painted, he barked out the new names, for his secretary
    to record, and imagined
red, white and blue Union Jacks criss-crossing the colonial
    skies,
over the walls of forts, towns, cities eventually.

"If there should be Peace," Lieutenant Governor John Graves
    Simcoe wrote
on November 12, 1790, "the new Colony will certainly require

an additional body of Troops."

The whirling eddy has spiralled its way downstream,
its anti-clockwise twirl now fifty feet past this dock.
The river's muscular current has taken over, surging down
 towards the lake.
The minnows have done an about-face. Now
they're swimming upstream, towards the falls, still
against the current.

Gerry 84

Tuning

Downstairs,
Francis, piano tuner, homing in on the
perfect pitches;
the sliding, steadying notes
resound,
resonate,
tremble the beams and two-by-tens, tuning
the whole house.

> Alexandra, 4, red velvet dress and sparkles,
> watching her daycare classmates, backstage.

This settling in
to pitch
from out,
this feat of balancing—not too high, not too low, but
just
right—this three bears
and Goldilocks recognition sends me 'way
past the consumer-mind of buying yet another
thing, the 1911 upright Heintzman,
for the children (not so long ago babies) to learn, to play,
and sends me to imagining them
touching the keys (A = 440 cps),
summoning with their fingers the sounds in their minds.

> Alexandra, backstage, before the children's
> Christmas concert.

And still, sounding, the harmony of that chiming:
tuner calibrating piano and house.

> "We're all so beautiful,
> we don't even know each other."

Birch Firecrackers, Killarney, May 24 Weekend (1993)

Birch firecrackers
    across David Lake
    by Iroquois Rock,
        supposed to be a cliff, but up close
        a slant.
Birch firecrackers
burst whitegreen
above the hills
    mostly red with spring
    maples
        blooming a bit late.
And the hills are white—not snow: rocks
    silver, shining silver from behind
    even while the sun stays
    cryptic, held
    in the Thunder Bird's eye.
Dark green silver, dark   green   silver—
    not white silver—
        as though the sun's
        light is tunneling through the hills—
        the rocks   green glass.

Gerry 86

Reading the Classics

Ah, yes: Plato.
Often mentioned, seldom read;
I'm reading some of *The Dialogues* these days.

Outside the murderers film themselves
sucking and flicking psychopathic blonde blue-eyed each
    others on tape;
freeze and chainsaw the corpse,
try to burn it in the neighbours' silo.
"Where's he gone?
Oh, just gettin' some more wood, eh?"

In the *Dialogue* called *Gorgias*, Socrates asks whether
"people who have learned things become such as that particular
    knowledge makes them?"
And Gorgias agrees.
"Then," goes on Socrates,
"the person who has learned justice is just."
"Yes."
"And, I suppose," says Socrates, "that the just person does just
    acts?"
How can wealthy old Gorgias wriggle out of saying yes to that
    one?
He can't.

Ah, yes: the Classics. From 2500 years of Greek
distance
Socrates
       bumps right into your face.
You know how you ought to behave, he states, aloud, don't
    you?
With that invaluable knowledge, your loving nature, your
    human skills,

your desire to do what's right—to be just—
your decisions are unmistakably clear then, are they
    not?

Socrates: gleaming postcard from the land of Knowing Better.

And a dream: friends, family, acquaintances, strangers, stand,
    look up,
        examining hieroglyphics chiseled and painted
        on the mighty stone columns at Luxor, once Thebes.
As I pass, tourist, nodding, they glance, then go back to
    deciphering ancient Egypt.
I am in a land three thousand years before Socrates spoke on
    the north side of the great sea.
Ibis-headed gods, winged, the sun a god, the moon, the Nile.
Pyramids where slaves became sacrifice.
Blood river.

writer

i sit here
on this page, curled up, back sore
as a friend was when i was 19 and kissed his woman

and i remember a line i wrote that same year
with shotgun in mouth, in my room of leaky roof
i jotted, "nervous as a christmas dinner"
i don't remember the poem i carved it into
and charles mingus, playing in my living room, is too busy to
    help

i wrote that line in a lonely september

and i met a girl at the university
and we got to talking
and we both wrote

so we drank to that, and to every other truman capote thing
    under the sun
and ended up at my place

that night in my chapel of liquor bottles
with their fruits snatched like some lied innocence
we made sloppy, unchoreographed love
and i read you poetry

and you listened with stardust in your eyes
and even though i knew you were a liar, i ate it up like Sunday
    ice cream

then you left

do you remember my sad doorway?
my candle wax spilled on the red rug?

two weeks later
in my sterile, thorazine-riddled writing class for two-time
    losers
my teacher
held up like the sword of king arthur, or the flames of hades
a stack of poems from her other class

and i remember you
lying on your back
arm over belly
fingers twirling red hair
telling me of your dreams
your hopes of setting the written world ablaze with your
    hidden talents
you wanted to be a writer so bad, wasn't that what you said?
that you would lop off a finger to have but one poem
    published?

the teacher read a few
and then the fourth one stuck me like an unsuspected nipple
the opening line read, "nervous as a christmas dinner"
i wanted to cry, i wanted to fight, i wanted to laugh
yes, i wanted to laugh, and did as i thought
well, now you are a writer baby
now you are a writer.

Laalo 90

saloon

come
run with me

to the
nearest
bar

and we
will
suck
on
bitter draught
with
parched mind
and
lizard tongue

and we
will
NOT
laugh
at the
souls of no hope
slouched
beaten
tired
at those
who have given up

we
will
be them.

Laalo 91

stick-up

tonight
i've misplaced my dignity
can't find my puppet-show pride

my humour was missing
but i found it under the sofa cushions with 27 cents in change

alongside the dried apricot hairballs under my bed
was my jukebox sorrow

my lust has been gone for weeks
i think my last attempt at intimacy took it

i plead with my patience to stop the silent treatment
try and coax my cold shoulder desire

all i find
as i turn tables and throw cackling chairs is my misery

behind the fridge is all my poorly timed trust

now
i
sit
beaten
on
the
floor

that first hint of victimization stings like a slap from a woman
you didn't even like to begin with

the cliché in me urges a b-movie shower scene
but i don't feel dirty
just a little violated

actually
i feel like a robbery.

Laalo 92

los angeles

2:45 in the a.m.
when you stare at a clock, the next minute takes a week
now, a week later, it is 2:46 . . . and one can relax
mouth scorched from too many cigarettes
10,000 too many cigarettes
and i cannot drink any more coffee or my heart will implode
as the lusitania of my psyche

and it is winter
and my feet are sore
were i a 40's film noir gumshoe, "my dogs would be barkin'"
but i'm not
and they are not
and it is winter
and i sit, hoping for a gunshot, anything to invoke some
curiosity
but i'm no cat . . . and it is winter

and i wish i were in a lounge
dressed in navy blue, a suit tapered to my own individual needs
with a rye and water in front of me
spring water preferably, as i can afford to be picky
change for a twenty?
don't insult me

and i swirl the rye with supple wrist
and i feel the iced cubes chiming against the sturdy glass
the glass stout, like a rugby man in a muddy dusk
and the rye boasts its way down my throat
bringing my face warm and numb
and i think the room smoke-filled
and jazz is played by a trio on a too-small stage
and their suits are rumpled and stained

Laalo 93

and they are sweating, dripping with a dour glee
while they blow and strum and rat-tat-tat

and as i tip-tap, tup-tup to the beat i am witty and sharp
razor-edged, ready for all comers

and i wish it were 11 p.m. in los angeles, which i guess it kinda
    is
and the sky is that deep, album cover, air-brushed blue
and it is 68 degrees with a slight breeze

but the building cracks or shifts
and this is northern ontario
and it is 26 degrees below zero
and my mouth is scorched from too many cigarettes
10,001 too many cigarettes

and jazz doesn't belong here, any more than los angeles does.

Laalo 94

hometown blues

today, the tuesday of my discomfort
brings more ice-cube glances from myself, onto myself

northern ontario summer
an aberration worthy of macbeth

right through the jugular of this cadaver city
town of lost fabric
village of no prayer

there is a street, named paris

here we mine for nickel
no romantic struggles for gold or lust for dark women

here we vote socialist
yet our social life is confined to fenced in, prisoned in
barbecues

karl was no relation to zeppo
the true humour in that whimpers away into the night
on a red-eye bound for montreal

here we paint plaid ducks
sulphurous sunsets and myopic moons

picasso is the name of a man who painted, that is all

a. y. jackson painted here, about ten miles from where i sit
the group of seven deadly sins

one of his pictures supports my wall
i wonder what they know of him in paris

Laalo 95

here we build smokestacks
our eiffel tower

here our cafés are smug because we imagine they should be

here we are rude, but not in a dignified way
here we wish we were AMERICA

here we know of no de gaulle
of no down and out

and i think of paris street
and i think they should change the name of that street

this city has nothing to do with paris
and then i realize
it is paris that has nothing to do with here.

Laalo 96

just not bolshevik

i sit alone, but not lonely
and there is no traffic outside
no wandering silhouettes
sexy silhouettes even
and moody jazz plays . . . low
for my baby sleeps

and i sit here
on guard for thee
sipping coffee
savouring cigarettes
in a room that was once black
but mine eyes now tell of a pale grey
and i can see things
that i couldn't see only ten minutes ago

and i am free and easy
pondering sometimes, but mostly not
there are no lights inside or out
quiet as a frozen lake on new year's day i would say
were i in the mood for speaking

but i leave that to the jazz
and i suck in the smoke
and let it out with a slumped motion
that is called a sigh
but it's not what i did

i just blow the smoke
and drink my hot coffee
and peer between the blinds

soon i'll go to bed
i'm tired of waiting

i guess there'll be no revolution tonight.

Laalo 97

Arthur Quesnel

Silence

is . . .
the emptiness at
three o'clock
on a hot summer afternoon
in a cathedral . . .
with the candles praying
in the corners . . . and making
wet with shadows the pastel faces
of statues
that stare dumbly back
at you
saying nothing
with paralyzed fingers
pointing upward
and robes
that do not flow
and sheep
that do not bleat.

Quesnel 98

I Don't Have The Time

I don't have the time!
I would love you madly right now, but
I don't have the time.
I must run to the museum
Before they knock it down
With their machines
To make room for the casino.

I don't have the time!
The Fire Department has set
The Library ablaze and the books
Have not been removed.
They didn't have the time.

Bury the sound system
And hide the music.
The orchestras have been outlawed
And the concert halls too
By the black-shirted execs
Who need more room for banking.

They've dammed up the rivers.
The lakes have gone dry.
The babel, from the towers
As high as the sky,
Is that Religion's a fraud
And the priests all must die.

I would sit down and talk
But I don't have the time.
I must steal to the narrow wood
To listen to the bird
Before it flies north,
Where the ice has gone
Below the green-grey sky
That is falling . . .
This time for real.

Quesnel 99

Country

I asked Gabby,
"What's the difference between
A jig, a reel and a hoedown?".
He answered at great length,
At great length,
Straining for exactitude.
I listened deferentially.
He was seven years older than I
And an expert.
I realize now that
He didn't know
What the hell he was talking about.
But at the time I didn't know.
I really wanted to know.

Wolf

How dare you hobble into my backyard
And into my life,
Bundling down heavily, resting painfully,
Crossing my path.

I won't disturb you.

At a distance, you stare at me warily.
Don't move.
You know I can be trusted.

Stay for as long as you want.
I'll portion out a corner
For you to spend your days.
I am no Prince
And you no Fox,
But I'm sure we'll get along,
Respectfully keeping our distances,
At least for now . . .

One of us,
Out of jealous fear and ignorance
Of misunderstood beauty and wild independence,
Did this to you.

I feel responsible for your pain.

I dread your rising
And going off to some
Gun collector's backyard.

You do not have my visions
Of your head on a stick.

We do it to our own.

Morris Street

First street in my life,
Echoing still the footfalls
Of my lunchpailed tired father.
This is my seventh year
"La guerre est finie!" street,
Horse-drawn, milkwagoned,
Clotheslined and verandahed,
A first communion,
Christmas reunion street,
An aproned working mother in
An enameled yellow kitchen street,
A woodpile and coal scuttle and
Saturday bathtime street,
A yelling, crowded road game street,
A friend and enemy street of
Battles won and lost . . .
Of places to hide . . .
A fork-tongued street,
Venue of some kept promises
And of a not yet lived life
Of dreams and other streets.

Marianne Schafer

For Michael

I'd like to put my life on hold
In this moment of sunrise
On the way to Ontario
Warm light on my face
Through the windshield
Past new-ploughed fields
Two farm dogs chasing a deer
Children sleeping
Laced in each other's limbs
Dog napping beneath my hand
Mozart and
the fragrance of nectarines
You at my side.

Wholeness

I came to the island in May.
Winter's freeze, spring's thaw,
had ground my mind to gravel.
I was tired, nearly broken.
From deep within the dark of
the island's inner woods,
a place I'd never seen,
where wildness lived like a hermit,
healing seeped into
my seamless sleep.
Beneath a day-blind moon
I dozed in sunlight while
darkness worked
its ancient cure.

Later, I visited a nearby island,
Newly cleared and brushed
to let the wind blow through,
to make all sides visible:
trees reduced to
great piles of limbs,
charred remains of brushfires,
coarse grass covering bulldozer tracks.
I walked over emptiness
like an abandoned city lot
where all was known.
There was no healing darkness,
Only the open sky.

Bay of Islands Alphabet

Anishnabe, land of the aurora borealis,
Birches, bass, bears, blueberries,
    beavers and bell rocks where
Canada warblers sing in the cedars
    and the spirit of the Commodore still lives. From
Docks one can sail to Dreamer's Rock,
Europa Reef, any port in the world. Here are
Ferns and fireweeds and flags that saw
    Franklin Roosevelt and
Great blue herons.
Hummingbirds whirr among hawkweed and harebells.
Indian pipes and iris soften glacier-scarred rocks.
Junipers harden the thin soil. At night, in the glow of
Kerosene lamps,
Loon songs drift over the North Channel from the
La Cloche Mountains to Little Current, the air
    fragrant with lilacs and lupines. The sun and
Moon sparkle on water that is home
    to mayflies and muskellunge. Here,
Native Americans honor the old ways, speaking
Ojibway.
Pink moccasin flowers, pale corydalis, pike,
Queen Anne's lace,
Rugosa roses, reindeer moss and raspberries
    flourish in this rainbow country of
Spruces, stars, seagulls, sunrises, sumac, shoals,
    squirrels and sunsets.
Toads and terns saw
Ubiquitous, undaunted
Voyageurs who paddled canoes through
Water lilies of this ancient bay—
    a difficult passage for today's
X number of
Yachts with sails full of
Zephyrs.

Wildflower Honey

Amber elixir coats my tongue,
I taste the scent of lilacs and lupines.

Bottled gentians slide down my throat,
Breath infused with clover.

Queen Anne's lace permeates my curly brain,
All thought pink, like rugosa roses.

I hear the footfalls of lady slippers,
Low intonations of Indian pipes.

Pale corydalis strengthens weak sinews,
Each heartbeat flutters like clouds of trilliums

Crown vetch courses through arteries and veins,
Puffy bladderwarts light dark passages.

Sweetgrass and mayflowers perfume my hair,
Perspiration is liquid columbines.

The palms of my hands, the soles of my feet,
Are oiled with the warmth of St. John's wort.

Harebells cling to the connective tissues,
Waterlilies float in clear fluids.

And I am one with the islands.

Reunion

Like mayflies pressing a lifetime into hours,
the family came to Bluebell Island
to celebrate half-century birthdays
through the communion of
a meal served on glacier-scarred rocks:
the centerpiece a damp garden of mosses, lichen, wild irises,
a feast in fragrant wood smoke—fried potatoes, onions, pike,
bass, Oma's salad, candlelit cake,
cool winds warmed by open fire.
The sun sank into black mountains and
seagulls floated in a vermilion sky.
Then gifts:
a toy giraffe for the birthday uncle,
a cod gurgling jug to the birthday aunt,
sweetgrass and dreamcatchers for the fiancé
and cousins from far away,
a plush beaver for the infant bearing
three family names.
Later, in the cabin,
written histories of the birthday couple,
a song of aging, a cat story and
fifty years of family preserved on films
transposed to videotape,
where great-great-grandparents, immigrants,
smiled at their offspring--infants who pattycaked, splashed in
bathwater—
now grown, heard forgotten chants of
"Potchie, potchie," and "Siege sagen."
Sense of place in the family,
siblings distilled parallel experiences,
memories of childhood pleasures,
pain and suffering now recalled with gratitude,
each generation looking backward and forward,

One, two, three.
Afterwards, the birthday couple boated to their camp,
the uncle's spotlight scanning shores for markers,
dark water patting the bow,
mainland lights glittering,
Milky Way dusting the sky.

Great Blue

A walk along the water's edge,
around the island's curve.
Just beyond view, the heron lights.
I step carefully.
Last year's weeds crunch beneath my feet.
From twenty-five paces, we eye each other.
A direct look into a narrow face,
white, without expression.
Black-masked eye, bonny plumes flutter.
We stare each other down,
sun on impassive faces.
Air takes shallow breaths.
Dragonflies dance,
invisible frogs croak,
warblers sing.
Nose itches, thumb scratches,
head tickles, black pitchfork scratches.
Hunchbacked to my waist,
at attention to my shoulder.
We speak.
I, clucks and chants,
she a single squawk—
a slight squat,
then shoving off,
wings dusting air,
tips and claws nearly raking water.
Left behind on glacier-gouged rocks:
scrambled eggs with cream—
tokens of encounter.

A Lesson in Grace

I

The breath caught in my throat,
my mind shrieked and wailed,
"Oh God, what have I done!"
Exposed by the lawnmower,
four naked baby sparrows in
a cup woven of grass,
mouths open in silent screams,
blind eyes in bruise-colored bodies
that twisted and turned in the bright sun,
camouflaged but for their writhing.
They were unharmed.
With a trowel, I placed the nest
in the canes of a rugosa rose,
hid it with grasses, a pine bough,
and retreated to the kitchen window.
With binoculars, I watched
the return of the white-throated parents.
With wary hops, they brought food
and comfort to the young,
but the nest lost its balance and
spilled the babies onto the lawn.
Again, their mute cries compelled me
to return them to the nest.
Later, in the evening rain,
I heard a hopeful song:
"Sweet . . . sweet . . . Canada, Canada, Canada."

II

The weather grew cold, windy, icy mist.
Each day, I peeked and took joy

in their miraculous growth,
from the size of downy pinkie tips
to fat, pin-feathered thumbs.
I repaid the parents
for their liquid songs.

III

A week passed, and one morning,
while kneeling in the grass, I found
two dead babies a few inches
from the nest—no sign of predator.
With heavy heart, I dug a grave
beneath the cabin floor,
marked it with a stone, and
held onto hope for the surviving two.
Later, from the window, I saw
my dog shaking babies in his mouth.
I buried the last together
under the same stone.
Later still, my dog snapped at a mayfly
fluttering beneath his nose.
The wounded instinct native to wolves
is also in dogs.
So I cursed myself and all mankind,
ugly disturbers of the world.
I mourned the loss of innocence
in my perfect pet,
and wondered how I could bear to hear
another sparrow song.
Yet that evening, outside the window,
a sparrow perched in pine boughs.
Head thrown back, chest thrown out,
a gift of forgiveness in a familiar song:
"Sweet . . . sweet . . . Canada, Canada, Canada."

Michael Shain

a summer rain

the evening sky is many
shades of dark drifting
southwest across the lake
trailing moonlight
over open water

the rain has ended
the night air is wet with
incense of aspen and sweetgrass
rising from the woods
as from an altar
before the offering

on the willisville road

in the silence of the trees
that cling to the side of
great lacloche
beneath the shadow
of the white rock
the canopy permits a view
of the highway
cut through the hillside
most can only glimpse
from a rear view mirror
at such a place
where time is measured
by the fall of leaves
or another ring at the
heart of the oak

kathleen

"it seems like only yesterday"
she says, her voice trailing
as her brow knits
anew and the old mind
attempts to sort
the images that flow like
a brook and bubble over
moss covered rock
blending past and present
lost together as the waters
mingle and join on their
unceasing journey down
"when we had the farm and
the big willows" and
a little girl runs through
the grain with her dog
down to the river to watch
their reflections in
the slow moving current

old woman of silverwater

your home by road's edge
is leaning into the ground
the heart absent dry tinder
remnants of one forgotten in life
blue orchids to your memory
wild roses be your dreams

black spruce near the doorway grow
in the damp shade yard
and the moss is a shawl
around your shoulders

the wind and I may enter your soul
and spy at faded flower walls
old ashes in the hearth
and see shafts of cool light
tease morning jewels hung from
grey strands
and linger for a moment
at the unravelling

sleep will come with an autumn gale
your relics will return to earth
seeds of a prior time
not lost to one who
steals a moment by road's edge
to watch an old house
dissolve in the woods
blue orchids to your memory
wild roses be your dreams

a buzwah noel

thoughts huddled in the morning chill
beside the stove hands clasped
as if in prayer for the fire to take
glass frosted by night lit
by morning sun
exposing old patterns
intricate bursting with light
a meadow of winter flowers
to walk among and reach to gather
but which like memory
defy all attempts to harvest
old patterns once
seen with young eyes
remain long after
her hair as she knelt to sift the ash
the sizzle of salt pork
potatoes rolling on the boil
a tinfoil star
memory beneath the blanket
a treasure of rock candy
dissolving cold hunger into
one room warmth
and the light
seemingly endless
streaming through the pane
turning her flowers to ice

sheguiandah pow wow

sounds of the heart pierce
the dry ground
and stir the sleeping
spirits to join
the dawning circle

beneath a round of cedar boughs
the drummers cry the ancient
prayersong while jingle dancers
move in rhythm waves
of scarlet and silver

footsteps in the dust
driven to dance
by the tapestry of sound
woven of time and the forest
blanket of sorrow, shroud of dreams

by shore's edge the slender
aspen move in spirit
slippers of green and silver
shake and turn against the
blue chalk sky

Literary Biographies

Anthony Armstrong is a writer of both prose and poetry. Several of his stories have been featured in Northern Ontario newspapers. Over the past few years, he has participated in many poetry readings. He believes poetry makes connections that cause one to see the world in a new way. He received Honourable Mention in the Northern Prospects Poetry Competition.

Dave Bartlett is the editor and publisher of *Sounding Line*, a news journal for the Parry Sound region. He has also published stories in *Canadian Cyclist*, *Arctic Magazine*, *Caribou News*, and *Tusaayaksat*. Though he has written poems and lyrics all his life, this is his first appearance in print as a poet.

Jennifer Broomhead was born and bred in Chapleau, Ontario. She has just finished her degree in English Literature and Print Journalism from the University of Waterloo. These poems are her first to be published, and she is excited to be included in *Northern Prospects*.

Julie Cameron is a graduate of Sudbury Secondary school, and is entering second year at Trent University in Peterborough, as an English/Women's Studies major. She really likes Gustav Klimt paintings.

Monique Chénier, born in Sudbury, currently resides and teaches in Timmins. Her summers have been spent in Gogama for the past twenty years. She says, "There is no 'wild woman of gogama,' unless you count me. I love the north, but believe that people must constantly recommit to it; it is too easy to abandon." Her poems form one third of a three-woman collection called *NeoVerse* (Your Scrivener Press, 1998).

Robert Dickson is a Sudbury-based poet long associated with the Franco-Ontarian arts milieu through his activities in publishing, performance, film and translation. *Kaki*, a French language translation of the novel *Frog Moon*, and *grand ciel bleu par ici*, his most recent work of poetry, were both published in 1997. He won third prize in the Northern Prospects Poetry Competition.

Kim Fahner is a Sudbury writer who has published a debut book of poetry called *You Must Imagine The Cold Here* (Your Scrivener Press, 1997), and has recently completed the Humber School for Writers correspondence course. She has published in a number of poetry journals, including *Hook & Ladder*, *Kairos* and *Yield*. She has happily given poetry readings in Hamilton, Montreal, North Bay, Sault Ste. Marie and Sudbury.

Tom Gerry's poems have appeared in several magazines, including *The Antigonish Review*, *Pomseed* and *Germination*. More recently, he has written and performed rock and blues songs. Nothing he has written has become a hit. Yet.

Lorraine Janzen lives in North Bay, where she teaches English Studies at Nipissing University. An active member of the local creative writing group, Lorraine has published poetry in journals across North America. She won first prize in the Northern Prospects Poetry Competition, and is at work on a collection of poems.

Laurie Kruk is Assistant Professor of English at Nipissing University. *Theories of the World* (Netherlandic Press, 1992) is her first collection of poems. She won second prize in the Northern Prospects Poetry Competition, and is currently working on a second collection of poems, *Loving the Alien*. She was Chair of the North Bay Planning Committee for the League of Canadian Poets' 1998 (W)rites of Spring Ontario benefit reading, hosted by North Bay.

Trevor Laalo says of himself, "I write poetry as a search for truth and honesty. Not so much in others, but in myself. For me, poetry should be about perceptions, not accepting those that differ, but understanding and appreciating them. Never allow limits to be placed on ideas or on the words that communicate them. Writing is a last sanctuary for true, unadulterated free speech. This should be protected and exercised with vigour. In the words of William Burroughs, 'Everything is permitted.'"

Roger Nash won the 1997 Canadian Jewish Book Award for Poetry for his fourth and latest book of poems, *In the Kosher Chow Mein Restaurant* (Your Scrivener Press, 1996). Poems in this book also won him first prize in *The Fiddlehead*'s Poetry Contest (1994) and *Arc*'s Confederation Poets Award (1997). He is President of the League of Canadian Poets.

Art Quesnel was raised and educated in Sudbury, with a B.A. in English from Laurentian University. He lives in New Sudbury with his wife Blandine and two sons. After teaching for thirty-five years, mostly in high schools, he is now retired, and can sometimes be seen scribbling in a local coffee shop. He plans on publishing a collection of poems, and is also writing a semi-autobiographical work. His favourite poet is Robert Frost.

Marianne Schafer is an English teacher at Park Tudor School in Indianapolis, Indiana. She spends her summers in the Bay of Islands, Ontario, enjoying writing, reading, photography, gardening, and nature study. Recently, she edited an anthology, *Voices from the Bay*, that was published by the Bay of Islands Community Association.

Michael Shain was born in 1956 in Toronto, and has lived and worked as a lawyer on Manitoulin since 1990. He started writing poetry in 1992, perhaps as a response to what he perceived to be the singular beauty that lies beneath the passing Island landscape.